DESTINATION SPACE

STARS

David and Patricia Armentrout

A Crabtree Seedlings Book

CRABTREE
Publishing Company
www.crabtreebooks.com

Table of Contents

Stars

On a clear night, we can see thousands of stars. Each one looks like a tiny point of light in the dark sky.

Stars look tiny because they are so far away.

Stars look tiny, but they are not. Many are bigger than Earth. Some are thousands of times bigger. Stars are so large they create powerful **gravity**. Gravity holds the star together.

The Sun

Earth, the other planets, and smaller objects, such as moons, are part of our **solar system**. At the center is a star we call the Sun. The Sun lights and warms our planet.

The Sun looks bigger than other stars because it is closer to Earth.

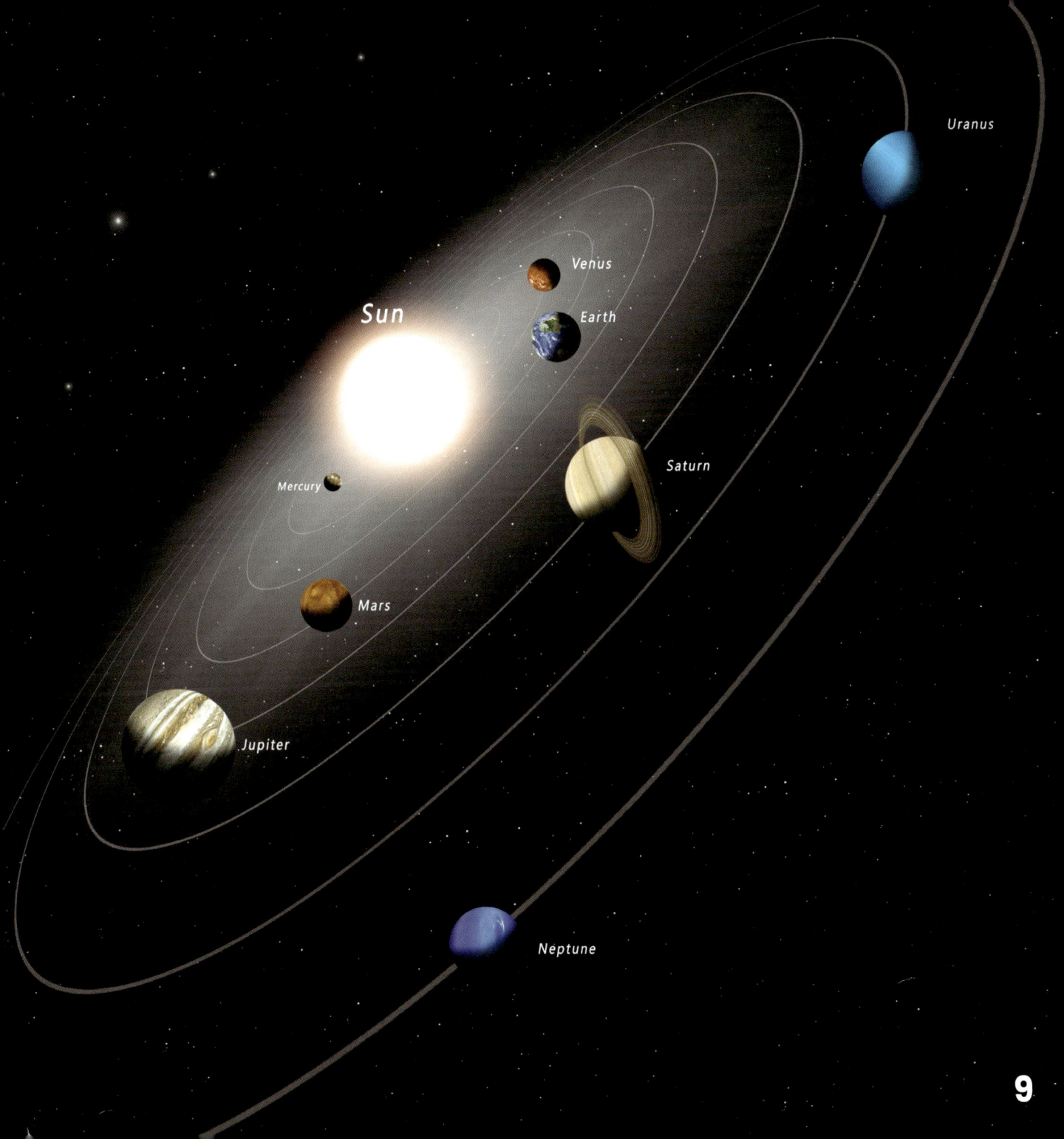

Sun

Mercury

Venus

Earth

Mars

Jupiter

Saturn

Uranus

Neptune

Stars are made mostly of burning **gases**. The temperature on the Sun's surface is about 10,000 degrees Fahrenheit (5,538 degrees Celsius).

The Sun is huge. More than one million Earths could fit inside the Sun. But in our **galaxy**, called the Milky Way, the Sun is just an average-sized star.

The stars we see belong to the Milky Way.
There are at least 100 billion stars in our galaxy.

Stars in Deep Space

There are billions of stars outside our solar system. They are so far away it would take our fastest spacecraft thousands of years to reach them.

Constellations

Astronomy is the study of objects in space. Ancient astronomers used stars to map the night sky. They used imaginary lines to connect and group stars. The star groups are called constellations.

CYGNUS

LYRA

HERCULES

Stars and constellations seem to move across the sky. That is because Earth spins, or rotates, on its axis.

LACERTA

TRIANGULUM

CASSIOPEIA

PERSEUS

CEPHEUS

CAMELOPARDALIS

AURIGA

URSA
MINOR

DRACO

LYNX

BOOTES

URSA
MAJOR

CANES
VENATICI

17

Ursa Major, or Great Bear, is a constellation in the **Northern Hemisphere**. Many people are familiar with the seven stars that form part of the bear. These stars are known as the Big Dipper.

Ursa Major
(Big Dipper)

Close to *Ursa Major* is *Ursa Minor*, or Little Bear. *Polaris*, or the North Star, shines at the tail end of Little Bear. *Polaris* is well known because its position in the sky barely changes. Since ancient times, travelers have used this unmoving star to help them find their way.

Ursa Minor
(Little Dipper)

Polaris
(North Star)

Ursa Major
(Big Dipper)

Stargazing

Stargazing is fun from anywhere. Find a place far from city lights for the best view. Computer apps can help locate stars, constellations, and planets. But, you don't need an app to enjoy gazing at the stars.

Glossary

astronomy (uh-STRON-uh-mee): The study of objects in space.

galaxy (GAL-uk-see): A system of stars held together by gravity.

gases (GAS-es): Substances that can expand to fill any space.

gravity (GRAV-uh-tee): A force that pulls and holds objects towards an object.

Northern Hemisphere (NOR-thurn HEM-i-sfeer): The half of Earth between the North Pole and the equator.

solar system (SOH-lur SIS-tuhm): A star and all the planets and space objects that travel around it.

Index

School-to-Home Support for Caregivers and Teachers

This book helps children grow by letting them practice reading. Here are a few guiding questions to help the reader build his or her comprehension skills. Possible answers appear here in red.

Before Reading

- **What do I think this book is about?** I think this book is about stars. I think this book is about finding different stars in the night sky.
- **What do I want to learn about this topic?** I want to learn more about identifying different stars. I want to learn what stars are made of.

During Reading

- **I wonder why...** I wonder why the Sun is called a star. I wonder why there are so many stars.

- **What have I learned so far?** I have learned that many stars are thousands of times larger than Earth. I have learned that stars are made mostly of burning gases.

After Reading

- **What details did I learn about this topic?** I have learned that more than one million Earths could fit inside the Sun. I have learned that astronomy is the study of objects in space.
- **Read the book again and look for the glossary words.** I see the word *galaxy* on page 12, and the words *Northern Hemisphere* on page 18. The other glossary words are found on page 23.

Library and Archives Canada Cataloguing in Publication

CIP available at Library and Archives Canada

Library of Congress Cataloging-in-Publication Data

CIP available at Library of Congress

Crabtree Publishing Company

www.crabtreebooks.com   1–800–387–7650

Written by: David and Patricia Armentrout

Production coordinator and Prepress technician: Tammy McGarr

Print coordinator: Katherine Berti

Print book version produced jointly with Blue Door Education in 2022

Printed in the U.S.A./CG20210915/012022

PHOTO CREDITS:
Cover courtesy of NASA, ESA, and T. Brown (STScI): Page 2-3: shutterstock.com/ ESB Professional. Page 4-5 © Milosz_G; page 6-7; ©shutterstock.com/ Heiner Weiss, page 8-9 © alexaldo; page 10-11 © Amanda Carden; page 12-13; ©shutterstock.com/ Stefano Garau, page 16-17 © Taeya18; page 18-19 and page 20-21 © Vector FX; page 22 © Sunti; All images from Shutterstock.com except page 14-15 © European Southern Observatory (ESO). https://creativecommons.org/licenses/by/4.0/deed.en

Published in the United States
Crabtree Publishing
347 Fifth Ave.
Suite 1402-145
New York, NY 10016

Published in Canada
Crabtree Publishing
616 Welland Ave.
St. Catharines, Ontario
L2M 5V6